Movies

and the

Moral

Imagination

Finding Paradise in Films

By Stephen R. Turley, Ph.D.

TURLEY TALKS
A New Conservative Age Is Rising
www.TurleyTalks.com

To all my beloved students at Tall Oaks Classical School, who have blessed me with the privilege of being their graduation commencement speaker for ten of the last fifteen years. The paradise I discovered in these movies is but a faint reflection of the splendor I've encountered in you.

Table of Contents

Movies and the Moral Imagination

We are living in the era of "faith-based films." Independent production companies such as Provident Films, Rebel Pilgrim Productions, and Produced by Faith are creating movies with an overtly Christian message and tailored specifically for Christian audiences. Even high-profile actors such as Nicolas Cage, Jennifer Garner, and Nikki Reed have starred in these films. And the business sector is taking notice: the 2014 movie *God's Not Dead* has grossed nearly $100 million in box office and video sales. It cost just over $1 million to produce. Needless to say, the faith-based film industry is booming.

And yet, while I certainly do not disparage these films, they do come at a price: faith-based films are a *marketable* representation of Christianity, not necessarily a biblical or historical one. The faith-based movie industry, like its music counterpart, has been created largely by secular corporations and marketing demographics. Branding a film as "faith-based" is obviously good business, but true to form in a formulaic and consumer-based world, it must be standardized and formatted to comply with the market research on that niche. Such movies evidence a Christian faith that has been dramatically reduced to appease corporate concerns.

But what if it turns out that the ocean of films that flood our theaters and Netflix accounts are already soaked with Christian themes but we've largely lost the eyes to see them? What if it turns out that the entire film industry, secular and non-secular alike, is itself *faith-based*?

As a cultural analyst by training, I examine the interaction between the various components and constituents of a population in order to discern and identify what precisely organizes people into a comprehensive social order. It's complex stuff, but at its heart is what scholars refer to as the "sacred." Originally formulated by the French sociologist Emile Durkheim and developed by the American ecological anthropologist Roy A. Rappaport, the sacred involves socially defined rules, understandings, and goals considered absolute and unquestionable. If a police officer were to pull me over for speeding, what do you think he would say if I complained that I didn't like that law? "Too bad!" comes to mind. That's because my dispositions, my likes and dislikes, are totally irrelevant to the legitimacy of a law. In this sense, the law defines me, I don't define it; it stands as absolute and unquestionable, so much so that I could be physically detained for breaking or violating it.

The important point here is that any kind of organized set of relations, customs, values, and practices must have a sacred link that serves as the basis for its arrangement. This is true of something as local and parochial as a Little League Baseball game as well as something as global and international as a United Nations assembly. And the reason for this is twofold: on the one hand, any set of social relationships and practices needs to have standards of normalcy, so that we know what to do in the various situations presented to us in that social order; on the other hand, we have to be able to recognize when that social normalcy is at risk or threatened. From this vantage point, it's been observed that the sacred in social orders functions very much like the immune system in biological organisms; social orders, if they are going to survive, need to maintain an equilibrium of power relations between the various institutions and structures in the social nexus, and be able to recognize when such an equilibrium is being threatened; otherwise, the social order simply falls apart.

For nearly two millennia, the Christian faith has provided the "sacred" for Western cultures. From our collective conceptions of God, cosmology, and morality, to our ordering of history, time, and calendar, our practices of welfare, healthcare and philanthropy, and to our cultivation of truth, goodness, and beauty in literature, art, architecture, music, and poetry, the influence of the Christian church had been incomparable. Distinctively Christian themes and conceptions of life were taught overtly in our homes and schools up to just a few decades ago; they were honored in our laws and courthouses, celebrated in our communities and localities, and proclaimed in our political policies and discourse.

And while recent events in Western culture are certainly characterized by an explicit attempt to turn away from such spiritual frames of reference, sacred themes embedded in a millennium of civilization don't die out so quickly. The sacred has a way of lingering in a culture, albeit often in mutilated and unrecognizable forms. The British journalist G.K. Chesterton once quipped that the modern world is full of the old Christian virtues gone mad; they've been separated from the Christian church wherein they found their fullest expression in relation to one another.

But we need to heed Chesterton's point: If the old virtues are still here, especially in our modern films, then perhaps the need of the hour is not so much manufacturing faith-based films but rather awakening the imagination to discover and discern such virtues in all films. What if, instead of watching *Christian* movies, we learned to see Christian themes and values in *all* movies? What if we cultivated such imaginations that could affirm the Good and discard the dreck?

But how? How do we cultivate such an imagination that can discern Truth, Goodness, and Beauty in a mass film industry that appears fixated on promoting values so diametrically opposed to the Christian faith?

The Moral Imagination

Such discernment involves cultivating within ourselves, our children, and our students what is called the *moral imagination.* It is a term first coined by the eighteenth-century British statesman Edmund Burke, and developed by such thinkers as G.K. Chesterton and Russell Kirk, to denote specifically the integrative role of the imagination. The imagination has been gifted to humans by God to perceive the divinely-infused meaning of the cosmos which provides a moral map of the world by which we might live our lives. This moral map is constituted by metaphors, analogies, and paradigms by which the totality of our experience can be synthesized and expressed in a Christ-centered intellectual, moral, and spiritual life.

The important point here is that the imagination is the integrative center of our students' minds and hearts. The imagination does not merely think; it feels. It does not merely know; it loves. It does not discern merely truth, but also beauty. An awakened moral imagination is nothing short of the awakening of the image of God within us.

A sanctified imagination recognizes metaphors, images, and themes distinctive to the Christian faith in all kinds of film, art, music, and entertainment genres that would otherwise go unnoticed. Not that such themes were intended by the art creators; most appear rather oblivious to their Christian origins. Nevertheless, as I stated above, a civilization so steeped and saturated in Christian frames of reference as the West does not lose such frames of reference overnight. Created in the image of God, movie creators inevitably leave traces of that image in their work.

I remember listening to a podcast about a fellow who took a walk in the woods with an ornithologist, an expert on birds. As they were walking along the path, the specialist asked him, "How many kinds of birds can you hear?" The fellow shrugged his shoulders. "I don't know, perhaps four or five." The ornithologist smiled: "I can hear about fifty!"

This keen sense of hearing is akin to what the trained moral imagination can discern in movies. The key here is teaching ourselves and our children to think of movies as a series of metaphors, to see the 'movie within the movie,' as it were. All stories embody wider stories; all characters personify archetypes. By teaching our children how to watch a movie, we are opening-up whole new worlds for them, worlds that bring the grand themes specific to Christianity into even greater focus.

Art and Virtue

The classical purpose of the arts is the cultivation of wisdom and virtue. And at the heart of wisdom and virtue is rightly ordered loves; the wise person loves what is truly lovely and desires what is truly desirable and thereby experiences human flourishing. The problem we are experiencing in the modern age is that the moral cosmos necessary for such a vision of art has been eclipsed by a techno-industrial age. And so, cinema-graphic violence, nudity, disrespect, vulgarity, etc., have all too often been amputated from a moral order, which makes discerning the moral value of films very difficult. Before the modern age, the artist intentionally sought to mediate the True, the Good, and the Beautiful in the artwork; today, we have to work to discern it. Cultivating a moral imagination is thus indispensable to fostering the discernment needed to love what's truly lovely in today's movie-making industry.

Movie analysis is central to classroom discussions with my students. Not only do I often illustrate my teaching points with relevant films, but the latest blockbuster provides ample frames of reference for rich theological and cultural dialogue. These discussions have been so formative for both student and teacher, that it's become sort of a custom for me to speak on a movie at the graduating class' commencement, which I've had the privilege to do for ten different graduations. Six of those movies are here presented in this volume. Each one focuses on the theme of Paradise restored in Christ, which served as a summation of my hope for each respective graduating class.

In terms of my own children, I've found that simply watching and discussing films with them is the best way of shaping their moral imagination. To that end, the six movies in this volume represent much of what those discussions consist; they are good examples of how I talk about films with my kids and students. And once you have taught them how to watch a movie, I find that they just take it from there. In fact, my oldest daughter sees things in movies now that I would never have imagined.

It is my hope and prayer that the following analyses of movies will enrich your imagination, and awaken you to themes otherwise hidden that provide a profound glimpse into eternal truth. May such an encounter transfer and benefit our children, as they learn to awaken their moral imaginations through movies, and thereby learn to live a life of wisdom and virtue.

CHAPTER 1

Inheriting Paradise:
Willy Wonka and the Chocolate Factory

Each year, at the classical school where I teach, I have the privilege of introducing a new crop of students in the upper school to the basics of an authentic Christian life. Two themes frame our initial discussions: Paul's proclamation that "all things are yours" (1 Corinthians 3:21) and John's admonition "keep away from idols" (1 John 5:21). On the one hand, Paul's redemptive cosmology celebrates the fact that the entire universe has been incorporated into the transformative life, death, and resurrection of Christ (1 Corinthians 8:6), such that everything the Corinthians do, they can now do as expressions of glorifying God as the all-sufficient provider for their needs (cf. 1 Corinthians 10:31).

On the other hand, John warns us that falling into idolatry remains a continuous risk in the Christian life. By "idols," it is widely recognized that John is not speaking here of physical images of gods and animals as used in pagan cultic rites. Instead, idolatry is seen more broadly as anything that takes the place of God in the affections and sentiments of the human person. Paul himself associates idolatry with "immorality, impurity, passion, evil desire, and greed" (Colossians 3:5).

And so, the Christian life can thus be summarized: All things are yours, stay away from idols.

But what does this look like? How does one faithfully fulfill this vision of godly living?

It's here that I like to share the story of the 1971 film *Willy Wonka and the Chocolate Factory.* Most of my students have seen the movie and remember it rather vividly. Which is good, for it contains perhaps the most profound retelling of how these two frames of reference – owning all things while staying away from idols – come together in the right ordering of our loves and affections.

***

Willy Wonka begins by introducing to us to little Charlie Bucket, a young boy who lives in a small town with his widowed mother and bedridden grandparents. His poverty-stricken life is bleak, but Charlie's child-like wonder remains undiminished. At the heart of that wonder is Charlie's fixation with the mysterious chocolate factory of the elusive Willy Wonka. The old and mysterious legend surrounding the gated factory is its magical qualities: how is it that the factory produces an endless supply of candy, and yet "nobody ever goes in, and nobody ever comes out"? Charlie's Grandpa Joe would fill his imagination at night with stories about the seemingly magical factory and the day Willy Wonka locked it up. "Why'd he lock it?" Charlie asks. Grandpa Joe explains:

Because all the other chocolate makers in the world were sending in spies – dressed as workers! – to steal Mr. Wonka's secret recipes. Especially Slugworth ... oh, that Slugworth, he was the worst! Finally, Mr. Wonka shouted, "I shall be ruined! Close the factory!" And that's just what he did. He locked the gates and vanished completely. And then suddenly, about three years later, the most amazing thing happened. The factory started working again, full blast! And more delicious candies were coming out than ever before. But the gates stayed locked so that no one, not even Mr. Slugworth, could steal them.

"But Grandpa," the wide-eyed Charlie inquires, "someone must be helping Mr. Wonka work the factory." Grandpa Joe agrees: "Thousands must be helping him." "But who?" Charlie asks bewildered. "Who are they?" Grandpa Joe leans forward: "That is the biggest mystery of them all."

The very next day, commotion fills the entire town. It has just been announced that Willy Wonka has hidden five "Golden Tickets" in the deluge of Wonka Bars that flood the world, and whoever finds the tickets will be able to enter the factory, receive a tour, and get a lifetime supply of chocolate. Charlie can't believe it! Could it be? Could he be one of the Golden Ticket finders and finally explore the magical factory?

One by one, the tickets were found by children all over the world. One night, Grandpa Joe showed Charlie a Wonka Bar he bought earlier in the day. "Go on," he implored Charlie, "open it. One ticket left. Now let's see some of that gold." "No, you do it," Charlie excitedly responds. Grandpa Joe slowly opens the wrapper, both of their expectant eyes fixed on it. "Something tells me we're gonna be lucky this time. I've got a funny feeling inside!" With a quick gesture, Grandpa Joe opens the wrapper fully, revealing the disappointment of a bare candy bar. "You know," Charlie says, crestfallen, "I bet those Golden Tickets make the chocolate taste terrible." Grandpa Joe wraps his consoling arms around the little boy, for grandpas, too, have dreams.

The following day seemed to seal the disappointment. It was announced that a young boy in Paraguay had found the fifth and final Golden Ticket. As the evening news reports it, Grandpa Joe demands they turn off the TV. "Well, that's that. No more Golden Tickets." Grandma Josephine dismissed their obsession. "A lot of rubbish, the whole thing!" "Not to Charlie it wasn't," Grandpa Joe responds defensively. "A little boy's got to have something in this world to hope for. What's he got to hope for now?" Charlie's mother believes it's best not to wake Charlie, but let him find out in the morning. However, we see that Charlie is indeed awake in his bed, overhearing the conversation, with tears streaming down his cheeks. "Yeah, let him sleep," Grandpa Joe agrees, "Let him have one last dream."

The next day, as Charlie was walking along the sidewalk, he noticed an ownerless coin in a sewer, glittering in the sunlight, which he picked up and used to buy a Scrumdiddlyumptious bar at his local candy store. As he turns to leave the store, Charlie thinks about his grandfather. "I think I'll buy just one more, for my Grandpa Joe." With his change, he buys a regular Wonka Bar.

As he leaves, Charlie hears a mass commotion. To everyone's astonishment, a newsflash reported that the Paraguay recipient was a hoax; there's still one more Golden Ticket left! Charlie, stunned, looks down at the candy bar he bought for Grandpa Joe. Could it be? Is it really possible? He opens the wrapper, and there, flashing in the sun light, is the final Golden Ticket.

Running home, Charlie goes through a dark tunnel underpass where he is suddenly confronted by a mysterious man with a scar across his face, who introduces himself as Arthur Slugworth, the candy making rival to Willy Wonka. "Now listen carefully," he said in a sinister voice, "because I'm going to make you very rich indeed. Mr. Wonka is at this moment working on a fantastic invention: the Everlasting Gobstopper. If he succeeds, he'll ruin me. So all I want you to do is to get hold of just one Everlasting Gobstopper and bring it to me so that I can find the secret formula.... Think it over, will you? A new house for your family, and good food and comfort for the rest of their lives."

As Slugworth walks away, Charlie runs home to celebrate his finding the ticket. He asks his bedridden Grandpa Joe if he would accompany him to the chocolate factory, and the wonder-filled Joe, in resurrection-like fashion, rises to his feet and begins to walk anew.

On the morning of the tour, Charlie and Grandpa Joe appear with the entire town at the gates of the factory. As the bell begins to toll, the crowd falls silent. The front door to the factory opens, and out comes a limping man with a cane and top hat, who hobbles along the red carpet towards the gate;

he stops, and suddenly rolls into a somersault and sticks the landing like a pro, and the crowd goes wild. He welcomes the fortunate five: Charlie, along with the gluttonous Augustus Gloop, the gum-chewing Violet Beauregarde, the wealthy and spoiled Veruca Salt, and the television-obsessed Mike Teavee.

They then discover a chocolate factory of wondrous delights, replete with lickable wallpaper, rooms that get smaller, and strange little men known as Oompa-Loompas, who live with Wonka and thus solve the riddle of how he makes all the candy without anyone entering or leaving the factory. But most magical of all, is the heart of the chocolate factory: a veritable Garden of Eden of candy delights, replete with a chocolate river running throughout its center. The children, both young and old, can't contain themselves; they run throughout this confectionery kingdom where everything is edible. They eat from whipped cream mushrooms, minty ivy leaves, candy cane branches, gummy bear hanging fruit, jelly-filled melons, and tea cup tulips.

But then, Augustus begins drinking directly from the chocolate river. Wonka immediately implores him: "Oh, uh, Augustus, please, don't do that. My chocolate must never be touched by human hands." His admonition falls on deaf ears. "Please, don't do that! Don't do that!" But Augustus wouldn't stop. "You're contaminating my entire river. Please, I beg you, Augustus!" Suddenly, Augustus slips and plunges into the river of chocolate. He's immediately sucked up into a large glass drainage pipe that sticks upward from the river like a chimney. The rest of the group watches helplessly as the plumpish Augustus becomes lodged in the pipe, building up enough pressure as to eventually shoot him up and out like a bullet coming out of a gun. Mrs. Gloop is escorted out of the garden paradise to find her son, who, according to Wonka, most likely landed in the fudge room.

This exile-pattern replays over and over again within the group. Each child gives in to his or her own temptation to partake of food that Wonka has not given them. The next to fall is Violet Beauregarde, who can't resist chewing an experimental gum comprising a three-course meal, despite Wonka's warning. As a result, Violet puffs up into a giant blueberry and is rolled away by the Oompa-Loompas. Then Charlie and Grandpa Joe sneak a drink from a concoction in the Fizzy Lifting Drinks Room, and float upwards where they are almost shredded by an exhaust fan. After belching their way back down to the ground, Charlie and Grandpa Joe reunite with the group in the Chocolate Eggs Room, where they encounter golden geese who lay golden chocolate eggs. The spoiled Veruca Salt, who coveted anything that someone else had that she didn't, launches into a room-destroying temper tantrum when Wonka refuses her demands for her own golden goose. She leaves the factory by falling into a garbage chute, followed by her enabling father. Finally, the last two children in the group discover Wonka's Wonkavision, a teleporting system akin to the way television frequencies work. The television-obsessed Mike can't resist himself; he forces his way onto the teleport panel and has himself transformed into microwaves and transmitted into a small TV shaped receptor, where he is reassembled but now only a few inches tall.

With only Charlie and Grandpa Joe left, Wonka instructs them to see themselves out and hastily closes the door to his office.

"What happened? Did we do something wrong?" Charlie asks. "I don't know," Grandpa Joe responds incredulously, "but I'm gonna find out." Charging into Wonka's office, Grandpa Joe asks about the promised lifetime supply of chocolate. "Mr. Wonka? The lifetime supply of chocolate, for Charlie. When does he get it?" "He doesn't," Wonka replied abruptly. Grandpa Joe doesn't understand. "Why not?" "Because he broke the rules." "What rules?" Wonka then proceeds to angrily scold Grandpa Joe in front of Charlie, accusing them both of stealing Fizzy Lifting Drinks and bumping into the ceiling which now has to be washed and sterilized. "So you get nothing! You lose! Good day, sir!"

Grandpa Joe can't contain his rage. "You're a crook! You're a cheat and a swindler! That's what you are. How can you do a thing like this? Build up a little boy's hopes and then smash all his dreams to pieces. You're an inhuman monster!" Wonka interrupts: "I said, Good day!" and orders them both out of his office.

Like the others, now Charlie has been cast out, away from the place that had become the heart of his wonder and awe. But Grandpa Joe is fixing to get even with Wonka. He promises Charlie that they'll take the Everlasting Gobstopper that Charlie received at the beginning of the tour to Slugworth. But something completely unexpected happens. As he's exiting the office with his grandfather, Charlie stops, turns, and walks slowly towards Wonka's desk. "Mr. Wonka?" Wonka ignores him. Charlie reaches into his pocket and gently places the Everlasting Gobstopper, Slugworth's promised "ticket" to Charlie's own everlasting wealth and happiness, on Wonka's desk, and begins to walk away. Wonka places his hand over the candy, this sacrificed token of promised prosperity, as if to offer his own embrace of the repentant gesture, whispering under his breath: "So shines a good deed in a weary world."

"Charlie!" Wonka spins around suddenly in his chair. Charlie turns towards him. Wonka jumps out of his chair and runs towards Charlie, lifting him up in his arms as if he were his own son. "Charlie, my boy ... You won! You did it! You did it! I knew you would; I just knew you would. Oh, Charlie, forgive me for putting you through this. Please, forgive me. Come in, Mr. Wilkinson. Charlie, meet Mr. Wilkinson." To Charlie's astonishment, Mr. Slugworth walks into the room. It turns out that Slugworth is actually Wonka's employee. "I had to test you, Charlie. And you passed the test. You won!" "Won what?" Grandpa Joe asks. "The jackpot, my dear sir, the grand and glorious jackpot!"

Willy Wonka is ultimately a movie about the object of our affections. What do we ultimately love? The gluttonous Augustus loved chocolate; Violet loved gum; Veruca loved anything owned by others; and Mike loved TV. They all loved things *in* the garden and in so doing, ate from their own forbidden fruits, seduced by their respective idolatries.

But what did Charlie love? The answer I most often hear from my students is that Charlie loved his family. But if that were the case, then he would have taken the Everlasting Gobstopper to Slugworth and solved all his family's financial hardships. Others have suggested that Charlie loved the chocolate factory. There's no question that he did, but it doesn't answer why he gave up taking an everlasting token of that factory with him. There's something more going on here.

What precisely was this test that Charlie had to pass? What was Wonka evaluating?

Perhaps the question is misleading; rather than ask *what* Charlie loved, we can inquire: *Who* did Charlie love? *Who* was the ultimate object of Charlie's affections and endearment?

The answer is found in the abandoned gobstopper on the desk: *Charlie loved the gardener.*

Wonka then brings Charlie and Grandpa Joe into a special elevator that he calls the "Wonkavator," one that can go sideways and slantways and longways and backways and, yes, frontways! But the one way that Wonka had yet to go was upwards. He told Charlie to press a special button, and upwards they went, up and up and up, so high that they crashed through the glass roof of the factory, soaring over their city. "Grandpa, our town looks so pretty from up here!" "Yeah," Grandpa Joe agreed, "look over here, Charlie. I think I see our house!"

"How did you like the chocolate factory, Charlie?" Wonka asks. Charlie couldn't hide his astonishment. "I think it's the most wonderful place in the whole world." Wonka smiles: "I'm very pleased to hear you say that because I'm giving it to you." "You're giving Charlie the--?" Now Grandpa Joe can't contain his astonishment! Wonka explains: "I can't go on forever, and I don't really want to try. So, who can I trust to run the factory when I leave and take care of the Oompa Loompas for me? Not a grownup. A grownup would want to do everything his own way, not mine. That's why I decided a long time ago I had to find a child. A very honest, loving child to whom I can tell all my most precious candy making secrets.

So the factory's yours, Charlie; you can move in immediately." "And me?" Grandpa Joe asks. "Absolutely. The whole family. I want you to bring them all."

Just moments ago, Charlie's fate appeared to be that of the other children: in loving individual things in the chocolate factory irrespective of the creator, their time in the garden came to an end. But Charlie was different. By placing the gobstopper on Wonka's desk, Charlie showed that he valued his relationship with Wonka more than anything in the factory. He cherished Wonka more than any material gain. And in adoring the gardener, *Charlie got the whole garden.*

Augustine made a helpful distinction between things that are *enjoyed* and things that are *used*. We enjoy things when we love them for their own sakes; we use things when we love them for the sake of something else. For Augustine, only God is worthy of being loved for his own sake, for he alone is supremely valuable. All other loves are subordinate to the love of God; all created things are to be loved as objects that cause us to delight in God.

Idolatry involves enjoying for its own sake anything that God meant to be used as a means of communion with him. Idolatry is therefore not merely wrong; idolatry perverts the cosmos. It orients the world away from God and towards the self. C.S. Lewis summarized Augustine's distinction well when he wrote: "Aim at Heaven and you will get Earth 'thrown in': aim at Earth and you will get neither."

I therefore see no coincidence that Wonka gives Charlie the kingdom when they are high up in the heavens. There, bathed in the light of the sun, Charlie and Wonka embrace. "But Charlie," Wonka admonishes, "don't forget what happened to the man who suddenly got everything he always wanted; he lived happily ever after."

CHAPTER 2

Thanks for the Adventure: *Up*

We moderns find ourselves living in a radically de-personalized world. In a globalized economy comprised of transnational corporations, centralized bureaucracies, and technocratic networks, anonymity is the new identity, and nurturing relationships of mutuality and love are easily lost. It is in just such a world that our priorities can become skewed, our ambitions misguided, and our notions of self-worth disfigured.

In the midst of our pragmatic and utilitarian age, a movie appeared a few years back that profoundly challenged such assumptions: the Pixar film *Up*. Released in 2009, *Up* is often depicted as exploring the themes of loss and the process of learning to let go that comes with it. I think this interpretation is sorely mistaken, bordering on such secular-inspired triviality as to make a mockery of the movie. Instead the film, at a fundamental level, does not call us to let go but rather to embrace the eternal significance of human relationship, wherein love awakens us to newness of life.

***

Up introduces us to a young boy named Carl Fredricksen. We first meet Carl when he is just eight-years old, sitting in a darkened cinema, wearing his WWI leather flight helmet. He sits in enraptured attention when the newsreel flickers onto the screen about Carl's hero, the famous adventurer Charles Muntz, whose motto was "Adventure is out there!" Muntz had returned from a year-long adventure on his special air craft, a blimp he called 'The Spirit of Adventure.' As he comes before the news cameras, Muntz presents to the world his great discovery, a skeleton of a giant bird Muntz called 'The Monster of Paradise Falls.' Carl's face beams with delight at the movie screen: one day he too will go off exploring the world's adventures for himself.

But then the announcer gives the shocking news: "The National Explorers' Society accuses Muntz of fabricating the skeleton!" Carl watches the screen, horrified, as the Explorers' Society removes Muntz's photo from their adventurer's Wall of Fame. But Muntz is defiant: "I promise to capture the beast … alive!" he cries out before entering back into his aircraft. "And I will not come back until I do!"

After the newsreel ends, Carl runs back home with a balloon in his hand, on which he wrote the words, 'The Spirit of Adventure,' pretending the balloon was his airship. He was buzzing and zooming with the sounds of the aircraft down the sidewalk, only to be interrupted by another voice in the distance, "Adventure is out there!" Carl turns and sees an old abandoned house and looks into the window. There he sees a young girl, named Ellie, who, equipped with her own WWI leather flight helmet, is pretending to pilot the Spirit of Adventure in the abandoned living room.

"What are you doing?" she cried out in response to Carl staring at her. "Don't you know that this is an exclusive club? Only explorers get in here. Do you think you got what it takes? Well do you?" Carl is speechless. "Alright, you're in. Welcome aboard," she says. Ellie takes off her helmet and shakes out here messy red hair. On the front of her shirt there were loads of buttons and badges. She unfastens one made out of the cap from a bottle of grape soda and pins it on Carl's shirt. "You and me, we're in a club now!"

In all the excitement, Carl had let go of his balloon, which had floated up to the second floor. In trying to retrieve it, however, Carl falls through a rotted-out floor beam and breaks his arm. And as he sits in his bed later that night trying to read, a blue balloon with a stick tied to the end floats in through Carl's window and hovers above his bed. Ellie's head pops through the window; "Hey, kid! Thought you might need a little cheering up." And the two begin to read Ellie's very own adventure book she put together. She pointed to pictures of Charles Muntz. "When I get big, I'm going where he's going – South America. It's like America, but south. Wanna know where I'm gonna live? Paradise Falls. A land lost in time." Ellie points to a beautiful photo of a steep mountain with a flat top, rolling trees and a flowing water falls. "I'm gonna park my clubhouse there right next to the falls." Then, she flips through the book until she comes to a page marked in capital letters, 'STUFF I'M GOING TO DO,' where all the following pages were blank. "I'm saving these pages for all the adventures I'm gonna have ... Only I don't know how I'm gonna get to Paradise Falls...."

Just then, she catches a glimpse of a collection of toy blimps on Carl's shelf. "That's it! You can take us there in a blimp! Swear you'll take us. Cross your heart! Cross it!" Carl crossed his heart. "Good, you promised, no backing out!"

And so ended their first day together, a day that would turn into the rest of their lives. Carl and Ellie, now young adults, get married and purchase their old abandoned clubhouse. They move in and restore it little by little each day. Ellie gets a job at the local zoo, and Carl does as well, selling balloons from a cart. And together they keep a money jar that has written on it, 'PARADISE FALLS,' where they would toss in their spare change. But expenses always seemed to get in the way: a new tire for the car, a new roof for the house, a cast for Carl's broken leg. But Carl was always determined to keep his promise.

Years passed.

And one day, on their anniversary, Carl, now an old man, decides to surprise Ellie with tickets to South America. But before he can, Ellie gets sick. And as she sits in the hospital bed, a blue balloon floats into her room from the opened door and hovers over her bed. Carl walks in, and sits down with her, holding her hand, for the last time. For the first time since he was eight years old, Carl is now all alone.

Unfortunately for Carl, his neighborhood is being increasingly torn down to make room for a bunch of tall buildings, and eventually, his is the only original house on the block. And, then, through a court order, he is forced to leave his home, their beloved clubhouse. That evening, he stares at a picture of his Ellie, and, with a determined look, crosses his heart.

The next morning, to the shock of everyone in the neighborhood, thousands upon thousands of balloons appear floating above his roof all tied to his house which miraculously lifts the house off its foundations and high up into the air and Carl flies away. With a smile of satisfaction, he looks down from a thousand feet up, takes out his compass, steers the house south, and Carl sits back enjoying his balloon flight to South America .... only to hear a knock at his door.

Perplexed, he opens the door, and finds a little boy name Russell, a cub scout who was caught on Carl's porch hoping to assist Carl and as a result earn his Assisting the Elderly badge. Carl and Russell become friends and eventually land the house in South America, just in sight of Paradise Falls. They end up running into and befriending the giant bird that got Charles Muntz in trouble all those years ago. Then, they meet his hero, Charles Muntz, now an old man, who has spent the last decades trying to capture the bird. But Muntz thinks that Carl and Russell are there to get the bird for themselves and so Muntz tries to kill them. They escape only to see the bird captured and taken into Muntz's blimp.

In the process of trying to free the bird, Carl and Russell have a chance to talk, and Russell reveals to Carl that his parents have divorced and he rarely sees his father. "My dad used to come to all my sweat lodge meetings. And afterwards we'd go get ice cream at Fenton's. I always get chocolate and he gets butter-brickle. Then we'd sit on this one curb, right outside, and I'll count all the blue cars and he counts all the red ones, and whoever gets the most wins." Russell pauses: "I like that curb. That might sound boring, but I think the boring stuff is the stuff I remember the most."

Carl and Russell finally rescue the bird by flying up into the air in Carl's balloon-floating house and intercepting Muntz's aircraft. In the process, Muntz is thwarted and Carl and Russell take over the aircraft, but at the expense of Carl's house, which they last see disappearing downward into the clouds. They free the bird, fly the aircraft home, just in time for Russell to attend his sweat lodge meeting and receive his Assisting the Elderly Badge. And it is Carl who is the one who pins the badge on Russell at the ceremony, only Carl pins on Russell the grape-soda pin that Ellie gave to him as children, what he calls "the highest honor that I can bestow, the Ellie badge."

The movie ends with Carl and Russell sitting on a curb in front of Fenton's, eating ice-cream and counting cars. And as the camera pans away, for the final scene, we get a glimpse of where Carl and Ellie's club-house landed: right in the middle of Paradise Falls.

***

As I think through this film, I see two kinds of physics at work. On the one hand, there is a seemingly miraculous and wonderful physics where balloons lift houses up into paradise. On the other hand, there is the physics of adventure. Adventure, like the balloons, supposedly overcomes the limitations of the world, it defies conventions, it transcends the tyranny of the mundane and seems to give meaning and purpose and accomplishment to life.

And yet, throughout the film, there is a strange tension between these two physics. The physics of adventure demands Carl and Ellie reach Paradise Falls and yet their house and circumstances prevent them from getting there. His balloon business hardly affords Carl the luxury of pursuing adventurous travel. And when he meets his childhood hero, Charles Muntz, the embodiment of adventure, Muntz in his blind ambition tries to kill him. The balloon motif throughout the film both draws them to adventure and yet keeps them from it.

And as I reflect on this tension, I can't help but think of our own age, this modern age in which we find ourselves, for we are in an age that imputes tremendous value to the adventure promised in success and achievement and accomplishment. We are in fact the first age that tells our young people: "You can do whatever *you* want to do, all you have to do is follow your heart and it will never let you down." There has been for the last several months a billboard on I-95 of British singer Susan Boyle which says romantically, "She dreamed a dream," and then exhorts us to "live your dreams."

This seems so innocent to us, as it did of course for Carl and Ellie, and yet there is something extraordinarily detrimental, indeed, as we find with Charles Muntz, even sinister below the surface.

C.S. Lewis described the difference between the modern age and the classical age as involving two fundamentally different orientations to the world, we might say two different physics. For classical man, the fundamental question was: "How do I conform my soul to the world around me and thus be drawn up into divine life?" The answer was through prayer, virtue, and knowledge. However, for modern man, the question is inverted; modern man is not interested in how to conform the soul to reality, rather modern man asks: "How do I conform the world to my own desires and ambitions?" And the answer is through power and manipulation.

And so, now reality is judged not in terms of virtue and faithfulness, but rather in terms of *success*, that is, how well one has actually conformed circumstances to his own goals, needs, and desires. Today, we have a class of people who are 'famous solely for being famous,' that is, people ascribed with celebrity status for no particular identifiable reason other than their association with celebrity status. The British journalist Malcolm Muggeridge may have been the first to use the actual phrase back in 1967 when he wrote: "In the past if someone was famous or notorious, it was for something—as a writer or an actor or a criminal; for some talent or distinction or abomination. Today one is famous for being famous. People who come up to one in the street or in public places to claim recognition nearly always say: 'I've seen you on the telly!'"

In other words, our age is unique in that fame is no longer linked to moral qualities, such as good and evil, but now solely through amoral categories such as 'new,' 'hip,' 'contemporary,' 'cool,' or my favorite, 'fun.'

There is, however, a radically dehumanizing aspect to this civilizational shift. For as Lewis notes, by cutting ourselves off from prayer, virtue, and knowledge, we have cut ourselves off from those frames of reference that classically awaken *love* within us, namely the True, the Good, and the Beautiful.

Love in the classical sense is a desire for union with the divine source of life, a desire to conform the soul to an eternal, transcendent reality that endows the cosmos with meaning and purpose and thus awakens our true humanity. In contrast, love in the modern age has been reduced to an emotive, sappy, therapeutic, even temperamental term that has

nothing outside of the self to sustain it. And thus our affections become highly erratic, impermanent, and promiscuous.

Moreover, there is an odd irony in all this; in that by attempting to conform the world around the self, we end up imprisoning ourselves. In the classical world, the purpose of culture was to act as a portal to conform the soul to reality; culture linked the human person with the larger cosmos filled with divine meaning and purpose. But culture in the modern age has a different function; it is used by the individual to conform the world around the self. And thus, culture becomes a kind of prison that surrounds us, absorbs and distracts us, and cuts us off from the transcendent, the True, the Good, and the Beautiful that awakens love and leads us to the divine source of life.

Up depicts well this imprisonment with Charles Muntz, whose slavery to his own ambitions for fame and fortune is evidenced by his life as a hermit living in a cave over the course of several decades. He is sequestered from humanity. He knows nothing of love or relationship. He can manipulate the lives of others, but he cannot share his life with others. And as a result of the absence of love, we find that this blind ambition has a murderous side to it as well, in that Muntz is willing to kill off anyone that could possibly get into the way of his desires.

And I think, too, of what we, as a modern culture, cut off from the transcendent source of love, have been willing to do in order to secure the success of our ambitions. In January of

2012, on the 39th anniversary of Rove v. Wade, then-President Barak Obama defended the practice of infanticide that has killed off over 50 million of our children because it "enables

our daughters to fulfill their dreams." When the desires of the self, success and achievement, fame and fortune, science and the state, act as our key values, we become not only vacuous and banal, but also indescribably cruel and violent.

Yet, as we see throughout the film, something is tugging Carl away from this physics of adventure and celebrity. And we see this tension finally resolved when Carl has been abandoned by Russell who goes on his own to help free the bird from Muntz, and Carl sits down all alone in his house now situated in Paradise Falls. On his lap is Ellie's Adventure Book. He opened it up and adjusted some of the pictures in the front, and then turned to the page that said STUFF I'M GOING TO DO. He sighs in agony, knowing that the pages that followed were empty, just like his promise to her.

And as he closes the book, he notices that there is a photograph underneath the fold of the title page, and so he opens the book back up, and, to Carl's surprise, he finds their wedding picture, followed by a picture of them together in their backyard, their birthdays together, their first car, trips to the park, their times at the zoo. The pages weren't blank at all, but were instead full of pictures of their life together. The last photo was of them sitting side by side in their chairs. They were old, and they were happy. And below the photo Ellie wrote these words: "Thanks for the adventure. Now go have a new one. Love, Ellie."

Carl suddenly realized that he did not let Ellie down; he kept his promise. Their whole life together *was* Paradise Falls.

***

For well over a millennium, classical Christian civilization understood that space and time had meaning only in terms of their participation in something greater, which gave them their eternal significance. The only way of making sense of the world and our human experience was by understanding the totality of creation as rooted in divine life and love.

Thus, since Plato, philosophy has understood that the love shared by two persons is an image of a loving desire for the eternally True, Good, and Beautiful. Classically, love involves an attraction, a gravitational pull that draws us upward to that which transcends our spatial and temporal limitations, and thus lifts us up into an indissoluble union with that which never ends, the divine source of life.

I therefore do not think it a coincidence that throughout the film, Carl embodies this physics of love with a gesture, the crossing of his heart. The cross is the manifestation of love *par excellence*; it is the revelation of a love not of this world; a love that comes to us not through success or celebrity, but rather through the brokenness of our lives. The cross is where God and humanity confront each other in the deepest and starkest of terms. It is on the cross that humanity is revealed for what it has become: when truth comes into a world comprised of lies and power and manipulation, it can only appear as crucified. And in that display of our madness, our violence, we see a love that knows no bounds, no depths too low; we see a love that conquers the world by being totally conquered, for the power of love is not the power of this world.

And what is the resurrection? It is the unquestionable display that this love is in fact unconquerable and inextinguishable, infinite in its abundance and eternal in its life; which in turn

awakens a comparable love within us and thus restores us back to paradise.

Herein lies why I reject the notion that *Up* is about loss and the process of learning to let go. *Up* has absolutely nothing to do with letting go, unless one is talking about perverted priorities and misguided ambitions. But these are the very priorities and ambitions fostered by a secular sense of self-worth. Instead, like the Christian gospel itself, *Up* calls us fundamentally not to let go of but rather to *embrace* someone. Both *Up* and the Christian gospel gift us with a profound truth: *paradise is not so much a place, but a person.* A life of mutuality and love is the ultimate adventure, and relationship is the ultimate and eternal promise.

And so, in the midst of all our challenges and our discouragements, all of our successes and failures, all of our hopes and disappointments, let us always remember and never forget: *Christ is Risen!*

The adventure has begun.

CHAPTER 3

Finding Our Way Home: *Hook*

If there were but a single word that could summarize those of us who dwell in this technological age, a good candidate would be: *distracted.* Every day we are bombarded with moment-by-moment news headlines, Facebook posts, Twitter feeds, Snapchats, and emails; oh, the emails! In fact, there are studies that show we now spend more than eight hours a day consuming media. Such are the perils of living in an information-based society.

The irony to all of this is that by succumbing to the blitz of soundbites and beta, statistics and data, we can all too easily *forget*; forget, that is, who we really are and what we were truly meant to be. Such is the theme of the 1991 film, *Hook*, the sequel to Peter Pan directed by Stephen Spielberg. A family favorite, it is a wonderfully profound window into the ways in which we can lapse into an amnesia of sorts in our technocratic society, but also how we can transcend all our distractions and preoccupations and rediscover who we really are.

***

The film stars Robin Williams as Peter Banning, a successful corporate lawyer whose relationship with his family, particularly his young son, is being strained by his all-consuming obsession with working his way up the corporate ladder.

Peter's career obsession, however, is temporarily interrupted when he and his family have to fly to London to visit his wife's grandmother, Wendy Darling, now aged 92 or 93. Peter is the featured speaker at a ceremony celebrating the expansion of Wendy's orphanage, which was once home to Peter before his own adoption.

However, the trip does not keep Peter from his phone, as he is in constant contact with the status of a multi-billion-dollar business merger. In fact, at one point, while at Wendy's London home, Peter's phone conversation is repeatedly interrupted by his children, which causes him to lose it: "Will everybody just shut up, shut up," he screams, "leave me alone for a minute, I am on the call of my life!"

But that life was about to change.

After returning from the banquet later that evening, Peter and his wife discover that their two children have been kidnapped from Wendy's London home. There is a letter, oddly pinned to the door with what appears to be a pirate's sword and it reads: "Dear Peter, your presence is required at the request of your children. Kindest personal regards, JAS Hook, Captain."

Peter is completely bewildered. "Don't you remember, Peter?" Wendy asks. "Don't you remember who you are?" Wendy informs Peter that he is in fact Peter Pan, and his old enemy,

Captain Hook, has returned seeking revenge. The problem is that the now successful corporate lawyer has absolutely no idea what Wendy is talking about, having completely forgotten his life before his adoption into a family at the age of 12.

And so, the situation requires the intervention of none other than Tikerbell, who flies into Peter's room and introduces herself. "Don't you remember me?" she asks Peter. Far from remembering her, Peter doesn't even believe Tinkerbell exists:

> You're a... you're a complex Freudian hallucination having something to do with my mother and I don't know why you have wings, but you have very lovely legs and you're a very nice tiny person and ... what am I saying? I don't know who my mother was; I'm an orphan and I've never taken drugs because I missed the sixties, I was an accountant.

While Peter is distracted by his own ranting, Tinkerbell knocks him unconscious and flies him to a pirate port in Neverland. There he awakens in disbelief, and is discovered by Captain Hook, who threatens Peter's children unless he accepts Hook's challenge to a duel.

Unfortunately, Peter doesn't have the slightest clue of what's going on. And, as it turns out, neither does Captain Hook. When Peter tries in vain to rescue his children who are dangling from a net high above on the ship's mast, Hook asks his senior crewman: "I don't understand. Why doesn't he fly? Is he not Peter Pan?" "He's Peter Pan, all right," his crewman responds. "He's just been away from Neverland so long, his mind's been junk-tified. He's forgotten everything."

Before Hook can kill Peter and his children off, Tinkerbell intervenes and convinces Hook to grant her three days in which to prepare Peter for their dual.

In the meantime, she brings Peter to meet the Lost Boys, those children who fall out of their strollers when the nurse is not looking and who have been collected by the fairies and flown to Neverland. These are the boys that Peter Pan used to lead all those years ago, but has since forgotten: "What is this?" Peter asks upon seeing them, "some sort of 'Lord of the Flies' preschool? Where are your parents? Who's in charge here?" The Lost Boys all point to a young man named Rufio, who dismisses Peter as an old man who has no hope of regaining his former glory.

Eventually, however, Peter begins more and more to remember his time in Neverland and at last realizes his true-identity. He transfigures into the spirit of a child, fierce and free, he remembers again how to fight and defend Neverland. And so, on the third day, Peter, Rufio and the Lost Boys storm the Pirate Port to save Peter's children, only to realize that Captain Hook has successfully brainwashed Peter's son to see Hook as a true father figure. Peter is crushed; he suddenly recognizes the extent of his neglect of his son.

Nevertheless, Peter and the Lost Boys launch a full-fledged attack, soundly defeating Hook and the pirates, but at a terrible cost; as Rufio lay dying in Peter's arms, he breathed out his last words: "I wish I had a dad like you." It is then that

Peter's son comes to his senses. "Dad," he says to Peter, "I want to go home."

Returning to Wendy's London house, the children are reunited with their mother as they celebrate the true identity of Peter. And in a symbolic gesture of his renewed commitment to his family, Peter throws his phone out the window. The film concludes with Wendy asking Peter if his adventures are over. "Oh no," Peter replies, "To live would be an awfully big adventure."

***

"Don't you remember, Peter? Don't you remember who you are?" This is an interrogation that is supposed to resonate with each and every one of us, a reminder that we all have forgotten something intrinsic to who we really are. That a story like Peter Pan would remind us of our collective amnesia is not a coincidence. The early twentieth-century British journalist G.K. Chesterton observed that fairy tales are in fact revelatory, that is, fairy tales awaken within us a remembrance of the wonder and awe that once filled our hearts when we first encountered the world around us. Chesterton writes:

> ... we all like astonishing tales because they touch the nerve of the ancient instinct of astonishment. This is proved by the fact that when we are very young children we do not need fairy tales: we only need tales. Mere life is interesting enough. A child of seven is excited by being told that Tommy opened a door and saw a dragon. But a child of three is excited by being told that Tommy opened a door. Boys like romantic

tales; but babies like realistic tales–because they find them romantic. In fact, a baby is about the only person, I should think, to whom a modern realistic novel could be read without boring him. This proves that even nursery tales only echo an almost pre-natal leap of interest and amazement. These tales say that apples were golden only to refresh the forgotten moment when we found that they were green. They make rivers run with wine only to make us remember, for one wild moment, that they run with water... We have all forgotten what we really are.... All that we call spirit and art and ecstasy only means that for one awful instant we remember that we forget.

But our fairy tale goes a step further, for it links this amnesia with Peter's being orphaned. For countless years, Neverland was Peter's home; but since his adoption he has found a new home, the modern world. This was not lost on the 92-year-old Wendy; when she found out that Peter had become a corporate lawyer, she remarked: "So Peter, now you have become the pirate."

Again, Chesterton offers us some insight here, for he believed that the loss of wonder was the key characteristic of the modern age. And this is because the modern notion of knowledge is rooted in rampant doubt and skepticism; one must, in good Cartesian fashion, doubt everything until one finds that which can no longer be doubted. But this modern conception of knowledge fosters a distinctively skeptical orientation toward the world; the modernist robs the world of wonder and awe precisely because he thinks he has the right to doubt anything unless it can be proven otherwise.

However, Chesterton noticed that, in Elfland, the orientation toward the world is radically different. We see this in what he calls the Doctrine of Conditional Joy, where all virtue resides in an 'if': "You may live in a palace of gold and sapphire if you do not say the word 'cow'"; or "You may go to the royal ball if you return by midnight." Chesterton notes that nowhere in the ethics of Elfland is such a Doctrine of Conditional Joy ever challenged, questioned, or treated as unjust. If Cinderella were to have the audacity to interrogate, "How is it that I must leave the ball at twelve?" her godmother might answer, "How is it that you are going there till twelve?" You see, because the condition is never more eccentric than the gift, no less fantastic, no more inexplicable than the wonder of existence itself, the child never asks, "How come?" This is because the child has not been taught the ways of the modernist, the wondrous eyes have yet to be blinded by the spectacles of the skeptic.

There is a wonderful scene in *Hook* that captures the contrast between these two pairs of eyes, the eyes of the imagination and the eyes of the skeptic. When Peter and the Lost Boys first sit down to eat their dinner together, Peter can't see the food on the table and on the plates. While the rest of them are enjoying the invisible food, Peter asks Tinkerbell: "What's the deal? Where's the real food?" Tinkerbell encourages him to eat up. "Eat what?" Peter responds. "There's nothing here. Gandhi ate more than this."

But suddenly, the food appears before Peter's eyes, albeit in a food fight with ice cream. Peter can't believe it! "You're doing it," Tinkerbell exclaims. "Doing what?" Peter asks. "You're using your imagination Peter!"

For Peter to remember his true-identity, he has to first re-imagine the world; he has to awaken to the wonder and awe, the Elfland, that surrounds him before he can return to his senses and remember who he truly is.

I don't think it a coincidence that the final moment of remembrance happened in the shadow of a tree. As Peter entered an underground tree house that was once his home in Neverland, he suddenly remembered everything, even his mother. But he still couldn't fly; he hadn't come yet to a full realization of who he was. This is because flying required both fairy dust, which he had in abundance, and a happy thought, a thought that is more precious than anything else. Peter froze, and in astonishment, it dawned on him: "I'm a daddy!" he exclaimed. "I'm a daddy!"

It was at that moment that Peter realized that Neverland and its magical wonder was not so much a place as it was a person. That phone conversation brokering a $5-billion-dollar deal was not the most important call of his life after all; the most important call of his life was standing right in front of him. His family *was* Neverland. Peter finally remembered who he really was; this orphan had now at last come home. And it was then, at that moment, that Peter began to fly.

These themes of re-imagining and remembrance profoundly resonate in the Christian tradition. The Bible itself uses orphanage language to describe the universal human condition. Our first parents were created as God's son and daughter, fashioned in his divine image, and placed in Paradise as their original habitat. But their sin expelled them from the Garden, and orphaned them from the paradisiacal nurture and care of God.

We, the sons and daughters of Adam, all want to go home, but we don't know the way. We instead turn to a fallen world as a surrogate parent, a substitute father, which indoctrinates us to see Pirates rather than Paradise as our true home.

Thus, the Christian story recognizes that in order for us to remember who we truly are, sons and daughters of God, we have to re-imagine our world so as to find our way back. And so, it was when Jesus and his disciples ate supper together for the last time that he told them: "In my Father's house, there are many rooms, and I go to prepare a place for you. If I go and prepare a place for you, I will come again and receive you to Myself, that where I am, there you may be also. And you know the way where I am going." Thomas said to Him, "Lord, we do not know where You are going, how do we know the way?" Jesus said to him, "I am the way" (John 14:2-6).

Hence the thief in the shadow of the cross had but one request of Jesus: "Remember me when you come into your kingdom" (Luke 23:42). The one to whom Jesus said, "You will be with me in Paradise," is the one who recognized that Jesus *is* Paradise. The cross is the Tree of Life restored; our tree by which we remember who we really are, inviting us back to the rivers of Eden renewed in the waters of baptism, and to the great banquet of bread and wine where we hear the refrain: "Remember me."

***

Here, in the midst of our noisy, clanging, pinging, and interrupting world, we can see the startling significance of Christian worship: our liturgies invite us to re-imagine the world as redeemed in Christ, and in so doing, to rediscover ourselves in Neverland, our original and everlasting home. It is through worship that we begin to see the banquet feast prepared for us; we taste and see, and we remember; we remember our God who has created us and redeemed us; and in so doing, we remember who we really are and what we were always meant to be: sons and daughters of Adam renewed.

CHAPTER 4

Run and Run Well: *Forrest Gump*

My boys line up across an invisible horizontal line in a field along with dozens of other runners, all anticipating the sound of the starting pistol. Their weeks of training have come down to this, the first cross country race of the season. I take my place along the side of their route, lined up with equally excited and supportive parents.

For well over a decade, my four children have been involved in sports. Tennis, gymnastics, wrestling, little league baseball, cross country, and volleyball events and competition have all featured prominently in our family schedule. Watching them compete has been one of the most joyous yet arduous experiences for me. Tracking their every move on the court or field, emotionally rising and falling with them, my hands shaking, fist pumping; in one sense, I felt like I was out there with them.

And yet, in the midst of all the excitement and disappointment in the hills and valleys of sports competition, we can all too often forget the profound significance that sport has for the Christian life. Far from simply an occasion for entertainment or self-aggrandizement, athletic practice and competition can uniquely reveal eternal visions of life that far exceed the competition itself.

Few films have awakened me to the profound spiritual significance of athletic ideals as has the 1994 film *Forrest Gump* starring Tom Hanks. While the film has certainly received its share of critical acclaim, I've yet to run across reviews and commentary that have done justice to its rich spiritual and athletic complexity.

***

The movie depicts several decades in the life of one Forrest Gump, a slow-witted but magnanimously kind and generous man from Alabama, who witnesses, and in some cases even influences, some of the defining events of the latter half of the 20th century. The film begins with the camera focused on a single white feather mystically blowing in the wind across a beautiful blue sky and falling at the feet of Forrest, who's sitting at a bus stop in Savannah, Georgia in the early 1980s. Forrest picks up the feather and puts it in a book he carried in his hands, a copy of *Curious George*. As a woman sits next to him on the bus stop bench, he offers her a chocolate from a gift box, uttering the now iconic words: "My momma always said, 'Life was like a box of chocolates. You never know what you're gonna get.'" He then proceeds to narrate the story of his sweet and unpredictable life.

His story begins in a doctor's office; he's being fitted with orthopedic shoes and metal leg braces. As the doctor sets him down on his feet, the little boy clanks stiffly around the room.

"His legs are strong," the doctor tells his mother, "but his back is as crooked as a politician."

Forrest's mother is his greatest advocate; she makes every effort to ensure his success, and teaches him wise proverbs which Forrest repeats throughout his life.

On his first day of school, back in 1954, he recounts how the children reacted when he awkwardly boarded the school bus: no one was letting him sit next to them. As he hopelessly gimped along the aisle, all of a sudden, he heard a gentle sweet voice: "You can sit here if you want." Forrest turned and stared into the eyes of little Jenny Curran, just his age. "I had never seen anything so beautiful in my life," the older Forrest recollects. "She was like an angel."

Jenny and Forrest became best of friends. "We was like peas and carrots," Forrest repeatedly recalled. She taught Forrest how to climb a tree and read a book, indeed, from the very book, *Curious George*.

But Forrest soon learned of Jenny's dark secret. Her father abused her and her sister physically and sexually. At one point, when Forrest came to her home, she grabbed him by the hand as they ran into her father's corn field. She and Forrest kneeled down underneath the shelter of the cornstalks as her father called after her in a drunken rage. "Pray with me, Forrest. Pray with me." And she began to pray out loud over and over again: "Dear God, make me a bird so I can fly far, far, far away from here."

The next day, as she and Forrest were walking along a path, a dirt clod hit Forrest in the back of the head. A group of boys on their bikes came up from behind and began harassing Forrest. In the hail of dirt clods, Jenny cries out: "Run, Forrest, run!" He tries to run along the path, but his braces make it impossible. He awkwardly hobbles along as the boys begin to chase him. "Run Forrest! Run away!" Jenny cried. Forrest looks over his shoulder; the boys on the bikes peddle faster as they gain on him. But all of a sudden, his braces begin to shatter, sending metal and plastic flying into the air; he runs faster and faster until his metal braces fly completely off his legs, and to his joyful astonishment, he could outrun even the boys on their bikes.

Forrest grew up to be one of the fastest runners in Alabama, so fast that his lightning speed gets him into college on a football scholarship. He later became an All-American, and got to go to the White House and meet then President Kennedy.

Jenny, too, went off to college, and Forrest would go to visit her every chance he got. After his college graduation, Forrest enlists in the army and is sent to Vietnam. On his way, he makes fast friends with a young black man named Bubba, who worked on a shrimp boat all his life. Bubba convinces Forrest to go into the shrimping business with him when the war is over. In the meantime, both Forrest and Bubba come under the command of one Lt. Dan Taylor, who's swashbuckling bravado exemplified a long family military tradition. "You stick with me," Dan exhorts, "you learn from the guys who been in the country awhile, you'll be alright."

Alas, this was not to be. While on patrol, Forrest's platoon is attacked. Though Forrest rescues many of them, Bubba is killed in action and Lt. Dan loses both of his legs in a blast. After spending time in the hospital to treat his own wounds, Forrest returns to the US and is awarded the Congressional Medal of Honor.

While in DC for the award, Forrest reunites with Jenny at an anti-war rally that he happens to stumble upon. It turns out that in the intervening years Jenny was kicked out of college and was travelling from place to place, working at strip bars and living a drug-infested countercultural life. Forrest encourages her to come back with him to Alabama, but Jenny shakes her head; "Forrest," she says, "we have very, very different lives." Forrest pulls his Medal of Honor from around his neck and gives it to Jenny. She looks at him in unbelief: "Why are you so good to me?" Forrest looked surprised: "Cause you're my girl." Jenny smiled: "I'll always be your girl, Forrest."

Returning home, Forrest is offered an endorsement from a company that makes ping-pong paddles. As it turns out, while in the hospital, Forrest learned that he had an amazing talent for ping pong. The endorsement paid him $25,000, which he uses to buy a shrimping boat, fulfilling his promise to Bubba. His commanding officer from Vietnam, Lieutenant Dan, joins Forrest, but Dan's not the same. Since coming back from Vietnam, he's coped with his wheelchair bound life with nothing but drugs and alcohol.

We get a glimpse of the storm that raged within Lt. Dan's soul with the coming of Hurricane Carmen. Their ship was the only shrimp boat to ride the storm throughout the night. Dan screams out and challenges and curses God in the midst of the storm to try and sink the boat. But instead, the morning calm breaks in, and their boat becomes the only one left intact from the storm and in turn monopolizes the Delta shrimping business, making Forrest and Lt. Dan a fortune. Financially secure for the rest of his life, Forrest returns home to see his mother's last days.

Then, to Forrest's surprise, Jenny herself returned to Alabama and visited Forrest. He pledged his love to her and asked her to marry him. Jenny declined, but instead offered herself to him in the way she had been offering herself to men throughout her travels: she spent the night with him only to run away the next morning. And so, Forrest, too, began to run. Seemingly capriciously, he decides to keep running and running across the country several times, over some three and a half years, becoming a media sensation in the process.

Having seen him on television, Jenny eventually wrote a letter to him, asking him to visit her. And that's why we see Forrest sitting on a bus-stop bench in Savanah. Once reunited, he discovers Jenny has a young son, and Forrest finds out that he's the father. Jenny then informs Forrest that she's suffering from a virus, and the doctors can't cure it. Forrest didn't miss a beat: "You could come home with me, Jenny ... I'll take care of you if you're sick." Jenny can't believe it; there was only one thing for her to say in response to such unconditional kindness: "Would you marry me, Forrest?" Jenny finally came home.

At their wedding banquet, the guest of honor was none other than Lt. Dan, who arrived introducing his own fiancée, and he was walking! "Titanium alloy," he says as he points to his prosthetic legs. He stood for the entire ceremony.

Jenny died soon afterward, and Forrest buried her by their very own special tree. The movie ends with father and son waiting together for the bus on little Forrest Jr's first day of school. Forrest notices his son clinging to a book, *Curious George*. Forrest opens the book with a smile, and the white feather we saw mystically appear at the beginning gently falls from its pages. The bus arrives, and as his son is about to board, Forrest calls out to him: "Hey little Forrest, I love you." "I love you, too, Daddy." The white feather is caught up on a breeze and ascends into the deep blue sky.

**

"Run, Forrest, run!" Jenny's exhortation resonates throughout the film. Forrest runs away from bullies, he runs through the football field, away from battle, across the United States. It's no coincidence that Jenny's last name—Curran—is derived from the Latin *currere*, which means "to run."

However, all the characters in our story run in very different ways. Jenny is running away from something, while Lt. Dan is running towards something. Jenny's journey is sporadic and random, flying from city to city. Conversely, Lt. Dan sees his journey to become a war hero as predestined and fixed, indeed, even entitled.

And yet, both Jenny and Lt. Dan find themselves frustrated in their journeys. Jenny's running from her abusive past only results in her running into more abuse and sexual exploitation. And Lt. Dan's certainty of his destiny is quite literally blown apart when he loses his legs in Vietnam, made all the more painful by the fact that he was rescued by this clueless nitwit from Alabama. In the hospital, he grabbed Forrest: "You cheated me," he cried. "I had a destiny. I was supposed to die in the field! With honor! That was my destiny! I was Lieutenant Dan Taylor." To which Forrest incredulously replied: "Yo-You're still Lieutenant Dan."

However unwittingly, Lt. Dan revealed to Forrest that he, too, like Jenny, was running away. One commentator summarized Dan and Jenny as both pursuing passions that were parodies of their true selves. They turned their hoped-for identities into idols, which caused them to run from and ignore the very things that awaken our true selves.

But Forrest's running was so different. It began with a kind of resurrection, the tomb of his metal braces and straps flying off his legs such that, as he years later recalled, "I could run like the wind blows." And herein lies the key to Forrest's running; unlike Jenny and Dan, Forrest wasn't running *from* those around him, he instead ran *for* them.

In many respects, Forrest's character is a variation of what's called the 'Holy Fool' in Russian literature, who's depicted as stupid, eccentric, and odd, but like the biblical prophets, he reveals truths about the people around him, truths that are often painful. As with Dan, Jenny resented this: "You can't keep doing this," she implores Forrest, "you can't keep tryin' to rescue me all the time."

But central to this rescuing are the ways in which the Holy Fool reveals to us our own foolishness; his deficiencies awaken us to our own shortsightedness and cripplings; his supposed lostness reveals our own alienations, our need to come home.

Lt. Dan, after his battle with God in the tempestuous storm, realized this. As they were on the boat together, basking in the post-hurricane calm of the morning sun, Dan looked over at Forrest: "I never thanked you for saving my life." Forrest looked a little surprised and didn't know what to say. Dan pulled himself out of his chair, mounted the boat railing and, with a smile, jumped into the water. Floating on his back, he looked up into the heavens and the eternal blue sky as his arms gently waded like a bird in flight. "He never actually said so," Forrest commented, "but I think he made his peace with

God." The next time we see Lt. Dan, it's at a wedding banquet; and he's standing.

For Jenny, as she lay in what would be her deathbed in their home together, Forrest brings her breakfast on a tray, he opens a window to allow the morning breeze to fragrance the room, and sits beside her. "Were you scared in Vietnam, Forrest?" Jenny asks. "Yes, well, I don't know. Sometimes it would stop raining long enough for the stars to come out. And then it was nice. It was like just before the sun goes to bed down on the bayou ... There was over a million sparkles on the water. Like that mountain lake I ran by. It was so clear, Jenny. It looks like there were two skies, one on top of the other ... I couldn't tell where heaven stopped and earth began. It was so beautiful."

Jenny sighed: "I wish I could have been there with you, Forrest." He leans forward, compassion filling his eyes. "You were, Jenny, you were."

It was at that moment that Jenny realized the miracle of it all: Forrest *was* the answer to her prayers; it was no mere coincidence that the wind-blown feather landed by Forrest's feet; he *was* her wings; *heaven came to her.*

In the Christian tradition, the theme of running shares in the classical athletic ideals of antiquity, which sought to showcase virtues, such as steadfastness, courage, and bravery that gave each individual champion the highest honorifics and incomparable glory. The Apostle Paul, too, sees the purpose of running and sport in terms of developing virtue in the Christian life, but he radically transforms the ancient athletic ideal. He rejects its individualism, its elitism, and the lure of immediate rewards, the very things that Jenny and Dan were pursuing. Instead, Paul sees such vain pursuits as revealing that we are all in our own ways running in the wrong direction.

In the biblical narrative, God creates mankind to dwell with him forever in Paradise, but man in a very real sense ran away; and in so doing, no longer remembers the way back. But because God is life and love, he can't bear to see us lost; so God becomes man and runs in such a way so as to find us. And so, when he sees a Samaritan woman broken and abused, going from relationship to relationship, he sits beside her at a well, and he says: "I am the water of life; I love you, and I'll never leave you or forsake you." And when he sees a paralytic man that the social world of the day cast away as cursed and worthless, he comes to him, and tells him to rise and to walk and to come home. And when he stands before the tomb of his dear friend who had been four days dead, he cries out: "Lazarus, come forth." And when men in fear and cowardice and jealousy and greed spit on him, mock, beat him and crucify him, he said: "I forgive you." And when they buried his corpse and sealed the tomb, he burst it open with the springtide of his own resurrection, revealing a divine love that is inextinguishable, infinite in abundance and eternal in its life, declaring: "Behold, I make all things new."

Thus, the New Testament picture of running well involves not the defeat of one's opponents, but running in such a way as to carry others across the finish line, to bring them to our true and everlasting home. Paul simply has no notion of the antagonistic competition and rivalry in the human quest for honor and status. Instead, the virtue attained in running the race involves lovingly extending to others God's own orientation towards us.

And so Paul exhorts all of us, as he says, to "run and run well" (1 Corinthians 9:24; cf. Galatians 5:7), to follow a life-course that has been marked out by the shade of a Tree of Life in the shape of a cross, and thereby realize in our lives and in the lives of others a cosmic victory that has already been won.

Perhaps you remember the film, *Chariots of Fire,* about Scottish Olympian, Eric Liddell. He had been training for the 1924 Summer Olympics in Paris his whole life. And when confronted by his sister, also named Jenny, that he was spending too much time training and not focusing on his future missionary endeavors to China, Eric reassured her: "Jenny, Jenny, you've got to understand. I believe that God made me for a purpose – for China. But he also made me fast. And when I run I feel his pleasure."

***

I have watched my children both win and lose on the field and the court, but it's the defeats that have served as fertile ground for planting seeds of truth. I've often taken such opportunities to remind them that all our defeats have been absorbed in the cross by the one who defeated defeat and gained for us everlasting victory. As such, we can rejoice with those who come out victorious, for their triumph is a reminder of the triumph that belongs to all of us, that is ours by right of our baptisms. Whether our team or that of our opponent wins, such winning should always remind us of the victory that belongs to us every moment of our lives. As Athanasius said, when Christ appeared to be most defeated, his arms were stretched upward in a posture of victory, the permanent defeat of defeat.

My boys are at the starting line; their torsos lean forward over slightly bent legs, their eyes staring out on the journey ahead. I, too, take my place amidst dozens of parents all lined up along the periphery of their course. Anticipating the start of the race, our eyes briefly meet; I give them a thumbs-up, and recite a simple prayer: "Run, and run well."

CHAPTER 5

Rise and Shine: *Groundhog Day*

Today, we are experiencing nothing less than a renaissance of classical education. According to the Association of Classical Christian Schools membership statistics, there were 10 classical schools in the nation in 1994, today there are over 230. Since 2002, student enrollment in classical schools has more than doubled from 17,000 nationwide to over 41,000, and all indicators suggest that the next decade will be one of significant growth. And we are already seeing the effects of this kind of education. As of 2015, classical schools had the highest SAT scores in each of the three categories of Reading, Math, and Writing among all independent, religious and public schools.

However, could the recovery of classical education mean more than SAT achievements? Students are once again reading the classical texts and great books, reciting epic poetry, studying the classical languages, developing comparable music literacy and art appreciation, worshipping through traditional liturgy, and writing and orally defending theses. Through this renewed encounter with the highest forms of classical culture, are our students getting more than merely testing advantages?

According to the 1993 film, *Groundhog Day*, the answer to such an inquiry is an emphatic: "Yes!" The movie has rightfully garnered enthusiastic acclaim from the likes of both audiences and critics, as well as professors and philosophers. Few films have matched its combination of clever and sardonic humor with profoundly deep moral reflection. In fact, Jonah Goldberg of *National Review* hails this film as one of the most important movies of the last forty-years.

***

Groundhog Day stars Bill Murray as Phil Connors, a narcissistic weatherman for Channel 9 Pittsburgh, whose delusions of grandeur are expressed by his self-given nickname, "the talent." As the movie opens, we find Phil very disgruntled. He's been given what he considers an absolutely demeaning assignment to cover the Groundhog Day festival in Punxsutawney, Pa., at which "Punxsutawney Phil" — a real groundhog — comes out of his hole to reveal how much longer winter will last. Phil reluctantly travels to Punxsutawney accompanied by his producer, Rita (played by the beautiful Andie MacDowell), and his cameraman.

They arrive the night before, and Phil stays at a local Bed and Breakfast, wakes up at 6 am to the clock radio playing "I Got

You Babe" and the local DJ's greeting: "Rise and Shine, campers, it's Groundhog Day." When Phil comes out to the town green where the crowds are gathered, he sees all the

people excited, and Rita is caught up in the thrill of it all. She can't contain her enthusiasm: "These people are great!" she says. Phil replies, "Yeah, they're hicks, Rita." The groundhog emerges, the crowd goes wild, and Phil turns to the camera, and with an incredulous expression, comments: "This is one time where television really fails to capture the true excitement of a large squirrel predicting the weather."

However, if Phil thought he could make a quick getaway out of Punxsutawney, he was in for a rude awakening. A snow storm strands the crew in town, and so Phil is forced to spend another night in the same little bed and breakfast.

The next morning, the clock radio goes off at the same time with the same song "I Got You Babe" and the same declaration, "Rise and Shine! It's Groundhog Day!" At first, Connors believes it's a typical mistake made by a second-rate radio station. But as the day unfolds he discovers it's the exact same day – February 2nd – all over again.

And this is the plot device for the whole film. Everyone else experiences that day for the "first" time, while Connors is completely alone in his awareness of the day's repetition. Phil panics, he must be trapped in some kind of time-warp that keeps repeating day after day after day! But he slowly realizes that if there is no tomorrow, then he can, in effect, live forever *without any consequences to his actions*. So Phil dives head-first into indulging his adolescent self. He shoves cigarettes and pastries into his face with no fear of love-handles or lung cancer. During a drunk-driving spree, he declares "I am not going to play by their rules any longer!" He uses his ability to glean intelligence about the locals to seduce women with lies.

But the goal of Connors' adolescent spree is his scheme to seduce Rita with the same techniques he used on other women. But he can't do it. He fails, time and time again. She simply refuses to give in to his masterful seductions. And when Phil realizes that there is no escaping this time warp, that he is eternally trapped in a perpetual Feb 2nd, and that all of his pursuits at self-gratification amount to nothing, he comes to the end of his rope, and, in total desperation, Phil commits suicide, only to wake up at 6am in the same bed and breakfast to the DJ's announcement: "Rise and Shine! It's Groundhog Day." So he tries to kill himself again, and again, and again, and every time, at 6am, he is greeted with "Rise and Shine!"

And so, Phil interprets his situation as only Phil Connors could: he convinces himself that he is a god. But Phil was soon to learn that there was nothing godlike about him. You see, throughout the movie, Phil would turn a corner where an elderly homeless man would be begging for money, a man Phil avoided as if her were a leper. But on one cold night, Phil decides to walk the old man to a local hospital where he can get warm, and shortly after arriving at the hospital, the old man dies. Deeply moved by this, Phil would spend each day with the old man, [in fact he calls him 'dad' and 'pop'], feeding him at restaurants, keeping him warm, trying to get him healthy, but to no avail. Every night, despite Phil's administering mouth-to-mouth resuscitation, the old man would pass away. Alas, there were just some things that he could not change.

And it is at this point in Phil's experience that he begins to discover that what makes life worth living is not immediate gratification, or moral autonomy, or flippant cynicism, or self-deification, but rather encountering those things that give meaning and purpose to our lives. He begins to read great literature and poetry, he begins to learn the piano and ice sculpting, he helps the locals in matters great and small, including catching a boy who falls from a tree every day. In fact, all of Punxsutawney is transformed by the caring attention he gives to those in need. And his affections for Rita transform into a love without reservation and without any hope of his affection ever being returned. In short, the perpetuity of Feb 2 became an arena in which Phil's humanity was awakened. And the result is that Rita falls in love with him. And it is then that the cycle comes to an end, Phil wakes up on February 3, the great wheel of life no longer stuck on *Groundhog Day*, and he lives the rest of his life with his dear Rita ... in Punxsutawney, PA.

***

As I reflect on this film, especially with regard to Phil's original self-indulgence, I find that it provides a fascinating mirror for the modern age to which we find ourselves waking each morning. For the last few centuries, the Western world and increasingly the East has engaged in an unprecedented and frankly radical experiment in human civilization. We are in the midst of a collective social experiment that is attempting to construct a civilization based solely on scientifically observed cause and effect processes irrespective of any divinely-gifted transcendent meaning. Rooted in Enlightenment conceptions, it was argued that the enthronement of reason would finally realize what humans have hitherto for attempted to achieve through religious pursuits, but to no avail: wars would end, prosperity and technological advance would reign, and social and economic equality was finally within reach. The toll that we all had to pay for such promise, however, was that we collectively had to surrender the concept of meaning – what the Greeks called *telos* – as a reality divinely embedded in a created order, precisely because the created order has now been replaced with impersonal nature. But this was fine, we were told, since now we have the freedom to impart to life whatever meaning we as individuals choose to give it.

And so, it is to the self that our modern age has turned for meaning and life. Today, it is ubiquitously believed that the self needs to be cultivated and nurtured, and in this process of turning toward the self, there has emerged a sense of entitlement to self-actualization, and an accompanying right to charge with malice anyone or anything that would seek to stifle the self. The result of this collective self-indulgence is what researchers have called in a recent publication "The Narcissism Epidemic." The authors of this study have noted "a single underlying shift in the American psychology: Not only are there more narcissists than ever, but non-narcissistic people are seduced by the increasing emphasis on material wealth, physical appearance, celebrity worship, and attention seeking." How far self-indulgence has become a virtue in our culture was captured profoundly by Ralph Schoenstein in his article, "The Modern Mount Rushmore." Schoenstien writes:

> One day last spring I stood before 20 children of eight and nine in [a] third-grade class to see if any heroes or heroines were inspiring them. I asked each child to give me the names of the three greatest people he had ever heard about. "Michael Jackson, Brooke Shields and Boy

George," said a small blond girl, giving me one from all thee sexes. "Michael Jackson, Spider-Man and God," a boy then said, naming a new holy trinity... When the other children recited, Michael Jackson's name was spoken again and again, but Andrew Jackson never, nor Washington, Lincoln or any other presidential immortal. Just Ronald Reagan, who made it twice, once behind Batman and once behind Mr. T... In answer to my request for heroes, I had expected to hear such names as Michael Jackson, Mr. T, Brooke Shields and Spider-Man from the kids, but I had not expected the replies of the eight who answered "Me." Their heroes were themselves.

It is sad enough to see the faces on Mount Rushmore replaced by rock stars, brawlers and cartoons, but it is sadder still to see Mount Rushmore replaced by a mirror.

Rita, from our movie, provides the voice of wisdom in the midst of this national narcissism. As she watched Phil's initial infatuation with himself, she quoted to him the words of Sir Walter Scott:

Despite those titles, power, and pelf,
The wretch, concentrated all in self,
Living, shall forfeit fair renown,
And, doubly dying, shall go down
To the vile dust, from whence he sprung,
Unwept, unhonor'd, and unsung.

Alas, Rita's diagnosis has begun to manifest itself in our collective consciousness. 'Death' has become a recurring motif in our age. We now talk not merely of the death of God, as per Nietzsche, but now ethicists declare the death of virtue, philosophers talk of the death of truth, aestheticians pronounce the death of art, and our world is increasingly being referred to as a post-human age, noting that humanity has no inherent meaning apart from the meaning humans choose to give it, what C.S. Lewis called 'the death of man.' With no meaning, no fountain of life from which to drink, our cultural pursuits have begun to disintegrate into the dust from whence they sprung, unwept, unhonored, and unsung.

And yet, it is only when we in a sense return to the dust that the blossoming process of resurrection begins. It is fascinating that only after Phil Connors dies to himself again and again (in fact, he makes the comment: "I've killed myself so many times I don't even exist anymore"), he begins to discover something extraordinary about our humanity, that we yearn for a meaning and a purpose outside of ourselves; that we long for a beauty that awakens us from our self-centered slumbers; that our hearts ache for a life filled with wonder and awe. What makes us human is an insatiable desire to encounter the true, the good, and the beautiful in a life transformative way, a way that enables our souls to reach for and embrace a state of being than which none greater can possibly be thought. This is the classic view of what it means to be human, summed up in Augustine's opening prayer in his *Confessions*: "Thou, O Lord, hast made us for thyself, and our hearts remain restless until they find their rest in thee."

And so, Phil turns to the very same things humans have been turning to for thousands of years, those things that awaken the divinely infused meaning that is there. He turns to music and art because, as transformations of time and space, music and art transform us. He turns to literature since it is through stories that our moral imaginations are awakened. In the words of G.K. Chesterton, we read the Iliad because life is a battle, the Odyssey because life is a journey, The Book of Job because life is a riddle. And Phil considers the needs of others as more important than his own, since he discovers that it is only in losing one's life that we begin to find it.

But Phil has only scratched the surface. Standing in this ancient tradition, the Apostle Paul wrote to the Philippians: "Beloved, whatever is true, whatever is noble, whatever is right, whatever is pure, whatever is lovely, whatever is admirable – if anything is excellent or praiseworthy – think about such things ... and the God of peace will be with you" (Philippians 4:8-9). You see, by encountering the True, the Good, and the Beautiful, we discover the echoes of a garden, the shade of a Tree of Life in the shape of a cross, the rivers of Eden restored in the river of Jordan, that take us to the all-sufficient self-replenishing source of life, the ultimate human encounter with the Incarnate Son of the living God.

Groundhog Day is a magnificent film about what makes us truly human. In our modern age, so enamored with self-centered technocratic utilitarianism and political pragmatism, it is a reminder – perhaps one can go so far as to say a revelation – of the deeply formative significance of literature, art, and music for our lives. Like this new generation of classically educated students, Phil didn't encounter the highest forms of human culture to magnify his pragmatism or merely get ahead in the corporate world, but rather to discover the wonder of a life of virtue, to taste and savor the wisdom of well-ordered loves. *Groundhog Day* awakens us to what it means to be truly human, to recover the distinctively classical conception of the educated person, to rediscover the world anew, to rise and shine.

CHAPTER 6

Baseball, The Prodigal, and Paradise:

Field of Dreams

It's the beginning of springtime as I write; that time of year my two young boys take to the diamond-shaped field of the little league gateway into the dawn of summer. I often sit on a three-tiered bench made up of decaying wooden slabs set across rickety stands, watching these once toddlers turn into young men. While I have two daughters for whom a special place is reserved in my heart, it's during these moments that I often reflect on the unique bond I share as a father with my two sons. My own father died when I was only 11 years old, and that hole as left within me an indelible appreciation for the connection between a man and his father that shapes his life.

Perhaps the single best film that captures this special relationship between father and son is the 1989 movie *Field of Dreams.* Though baseball features prominently throughout the picture, I am convinced that this film is about far more than America's pastime; it is a moving retelling of the Parable of the Prodigal Son, but even more so, the grand cosmic drama to which that parable points.

***

Field of Dreams is about a man named Ray Kinsella, played by Kevin Costner. He lives with his wife, Annie, and a young daughter on a farm in rural Iowa. Ray is in effect a washed-up hippie; having inhaled deeply the radical idealism of the 1960s, he has only recently and quite reluctantly become a farmer.

One night, as he's working in his cornfield, he suddenly hears the whispering of a mysterious voice: "If you build it, he will come." This voice turns into a premonition of sorts: Ray sees a vision where his cornfield turns into a baseball field complete with floodlights and bleaches, and that his father's hero, the early twentieth-century White Sox outfielder, 'Shoeless Joe' Jackson, will somehow return from the grave to play once again.

Obviously, he discounts the reality of this vision. But the voice keeps haunting him, and eventually Ray becomes convinced that this is something he has been ordained to do. Convincing his wife, Annie, of course is another matter. Nevertheless, with Annie's perplexed blessing, Ray begins plowing under the crops, often with his daughter sitting on his lap on the tractor, which provides the occasion for Ray to tell her the stories his father used to tell him, stories of

Shoeless Joe Jackson and his alleged association with the so called 'Black Sox Scandal,' in which members of the 1919

Chicago White Sox participated in a conspiracy to fix the World Series. While his role was later disputed, Shoeless Joe was permanently banned from the game.

To Ray's surprise, after having built the baseball field, nothing happened. Time passed, winter came and went, and still, nothing. In fact, the baseball field so harmed their crop production that Ray's brother-in-law, a banker, tries to convince him to file for bankruptcy or lose the farm. Then, one evening, when Ray and his wife were arguing over their finances, they heard their little daughter say, "Daddy, there's a man out there on your lawn." Ray discovers that it is indeed Shoeless Joe Jackson, in full White Sox uniform. Shoeless Joe asks Ray if he could bring others from the disgraced team to play. "Oh man, anytime. They're all welcome here; I built this for you," Ray replies, just before Shoeless Joe disappears into the cornfields.

The next day, however, Ray again hears the mysterious voice, this time calling on him to "ease his pain," and again a vision follows: Ray is convinced that he must travel to Boston and, for reasons he knows not, take the controversial 1960s author Terence Mann to Fenway Park. Ray had learned that Terence's childhood dream was to play for the Brooklyn Dodgers, and the team's move to Los Angeles was one of the most heartbreaking moments of his life. Ray travels to Boston and finds Terence Mann (played by James Earl Jones), but he is no longer the idealistic radical of the 1960s; Terence has since become a misanthropic recluse who no longer writes, and who threatens to beat Ray with a crow bar when he comes to his door. After reminding Terence that he's a pacifist, Ray convinces him to attend a baseball game at Fenway Park, where they both shared a common vision to travel to Minnesota and bring back a young baseball player by the name of Archibald 'Moonlight' Graham, who played one game with the New York Giants in 1922 but never had a turn at bat.

After they arrive in the small town of Chisholm, Minnesota, they learn that 'Moonlight' Graham became a family doctor and died nearly 20 years earlier at a ripe old age. Again, mysteriously, as Ray was walking the streets at night, he found that he was back in time, 1972 to be exact, the year of Dr. Graham's death, and there he meets up with the good doctor, who confesses to Ray that while he regrets he never got to bat, he would have regretted it even more if he had never been a doctor. And so he declines Ray's invitation to fulfill his dream. But, as it turns out, the mysterious forces in play would not be denied, for while driving back to Iowa, Ray and Terence pick up a young hitchhiker who introduces himself as Archie Graham, who's looking to play some ball. He heard that there are some towns in the Midwest that'll find you a job so you can play ball nights and weekends.

While Archie sleeps, Ray reveals to Terence that that's what his father did for a while, working odd jobs just so he could play baseball. "What happened to your father?" Terence asks. "He never made it as a ball player," Ray said, "so he tried to get his son to make it for him. By the time I was ten, playing baseball got to be like eating vegetables or taking out the garbage, so when I was fourteen, I started to refuse. Can you believe that? An American boy refusing to have a catch with his father... Anyway, when I was seventeen, we had a big fight, I packed my things, said something awful, and left. After a while I wanted to come home, but I didn't know how. I made it back for the funeral. He died before I could even introduce him to Annie." "What was the awful thing you said?" Terence asks. "I said I could never respect a man whose hero was a criminal." "Who was his hero?" "Shoeless Joe Jackson." Terence looks puzzled: "You knew he wasn't a criminal... So why'd you say it?" Ray couldn't hide his remorse: "I was seventeen."

When they arrive back at the field in Iowa, there are now enough baseball players that have mysteriously appeared from the cornfields to form two teams, and Archie gets his dream, he gets a turn at bat. As the players finish out the game, they invite Terence Mann to see what goes beyond the cornfields, and perhaps that will inspire him to write again. Terence eagerly accepts the invitation. Ray wants to come, too. "You can't Ray," Shoeless Joe says, "You weren't invited." Ray doesn't understand; why is it that all around him dreams are coming true, except for the one who built the field? Shoeless Joe looks at him with a big smile, and points his finger over to home plate, and says to Ray, "If you build it, *he* will come." Ray looks and sees a catcher removing his mask, and realizes that he is gazing into the face of his father. Shocked, Ray remembers the second voice: "Ease his pain," and turns to Shoeless Joe: "I thought it was you." "No Ray," he said, "it was you."

Ray looked across the field at his father and marveled. "I'd only seen him years later when he was worn down by life. Look at him. He's got his whole life in front of him and I'm not even a glint in his eye. What do I say to him?" After introducing him to his wife and daughter, Ray and his father have a long overdue talk. "Is there a heaven?" Ray asks. "Oh yeah," his father replies. "It's where dreams come true." "Then," Ray responds, "this must be heaven."

And as his father turns to disappear into the cornfields, Ray calls out: "Hey, Dad!" His father turns. "You wanna have a catch?" A smile beams across his father's face. "I'd like that." And so, on this baseball field, Ray's dream came true; he found his way home.

***

I am struck by how beautifully this film portrays in a contemporary idiom the Parable of the Prodigal Son, but even more so, the grand cosmic drama to which that parable points, the cosmic drama of Paradise lost and Paradise regained. The baseball park is a paragon of geometrical perfection, carpeted with grass glowing as parrot green, cool as mint, soft as a cashmere blanket, framed by the breezy movement of cornstalks, backgrounded by the eternity of the stretched-out canopy of a fathomless blue sky; a garden of aesthetic delights that awaken the senses and cultivate the imagination. Shoeless Joe in fact says as much; he tells Ray when they first meet that after he was banned from baseball, he would wake up at night with the smell of the ballpark in his nose and the cool of the grass on his feet. "Oh man, I did love this game," he says longingly; "the game, the sounds, the smells."

But for Ray and Shoeless Joe, the baseball field involved an additional dimension: it was a place where they both knew life before innocence was lost. For Ray in particular, the baseball field was a place where he could commune with his father, who appeared larger than life through childlike eyes, but whose stature faded as those eyes began to change. The baseball field was perceived progressively as a prison, and freedom was found away from home.

And yet, while Ray may have fallen away from his childhood paradise, the ballpark never seems to leave him. Indeed, we see this 'hound of heaven' motif with all the characters throughout the film, uniting them in a symphony of redemption that is able to transcend time. One commentator writes: "Baseball is rhythm without time, the lack of clock rendering the events immortal instead of static. There's no running out the clock... A baseball game lasts exactly as long as it needs to, like a life time..... Baseball is the way our hearts wish time worked."

Terence Mann draws from this 'time outside of time' when he informs Ray that he will not have to sell his farm or the baseball field that he built, because it will be a field of dreams for more people than he could ever imagine. In an eloquent soliloquy, Terence proclaims:

> People will come, Ray. .... And they'll walk off to the bleachers and sit in their short sleeves on a perfect afternoon. And find they have reserved seats somewhere along the baselines where they sat when they were children... And they'll watch the game, and it'll be as they'd dipped themselves in magic waters. The memories will be so thick, they'll have to brush them away from their faces... This field, this game ... reminds us of all that once was good, and that could be again.

In the Christian tradition, Paradise is not a mere sentiment or therapeutic fable; rather, Paradise is intrinsic to our humanity. As our first habitation, the essence of what it means to be human is inseparable from an environment wherein every square inch constitutes love incarnate. It is in the primeval Garden that Adam was created to grow, to blossom, together with the flowers and the trees, to cultivate and to be cultivated in an everlasting communion with God. The 12th-century mystic Hildegaard was moved to say: "God created humankind so that humankind might cultivate the earthly and thereby create the heavenly." Centered on the mystical Tree of Life, Paradise is that place wherein we are most fully human.

When Adam is expelled from the Garden, having rejected his Father, an indispensable part of our humanity was lost. The Tree of Life was replaced with thorns and thistles, indicating a cosmos characterized by death and decay. Our senses in turn fell, rendered dissonant, discordant, and our imaginations shriveled up into a parody of our true selves, characterized by an infatuated love of the self. And all of our broken relationships are but echoes of our original estrangement from the source of eternal life.

And yet, while we have fallen from Paradise, the Garden in a very real sense has never left us. The created order that was to serve as the habitat that shaped and sanctified the human person has now been restored in the Incarnation of the Logos, the second person of the Trinity. Just as God formed Adam from the earth, so now the eternal Son of God, in the words of the Gospel of John, "became flesh and dwelt among us" (John 1:14), a New Adam, the unblemished embodiment of Paradise restored. Indeed, this is the classical significance of the Eucharistic meal, where the grain and fruit of the third day of creation are transformed into the bread and wine identified with the body and blood of Christ, such that creation and Incarnation come together to restore our communion with God and one another.

Therefore, just as our humanity cannot be understood apart from Paradise, so our true humanity is comparably incomprehensible apart from the cross, for the Tree of Life is restored precisely in and through the cross. The cross is where God and humanity confront each other in the deepest and starkest of terms. It is on the cross that humanity is revealed for what we have become: when truth appears in a world marked by self-centered dissolution and estrangement, it can only appear as crucified. And in that crucified figure, we see the very heart of God revealed, we see a love that knows no bounds, no depths too low; we see a love that reaches out with nail marked hands to welcome us back into his infinite embrace. And it is this love, unconquerable and inextinguishable, that bursts forth from the tomb the Eternal Spring of resurrection glory, infinite in its abundance and eternal in its life; which in turn awakens a comparable love within us, reorienting our senses and restoring us back to Paradise, our true and everlasting home.

***

As I noted above, I write this at the dawn of Spring, the time of year when fathers and sons take out their mitts and begin communing with a catch. It's the season when I take my place on that decaying wooden slab across rickety stands to watch my two young boys take to the diamond-shaped field. I, too, am decaying. My days of sliding into second base are over. And yet, there is something of magical waters here. Sitting there, gazing over that field illuminated by the late afternoon sun, my boys are transfigured into what, in many respects, we were always meant to be: delighted dwellers in a timeless garden, that place where our humanity flourishes. And it is there, when my sons look for and catch my fatherly eye surveying their immersion in this field of dreams, that I am truly reminded of all that once was good, and that could be again.

We smile at one another. Paradise regained.

Thank you again for purchasing this book!

I hope this book helped to awaken you to the Christian themes in all kinds of movies, which in turn cultivate hearts of wisdom and virtue in ourselves and our children.

If you enjoyed this book, then I'd like to ask you for a favor: Would you be kind enough to leave a review for this book on Amazon? I would so greatly appreciate it!

Thank you so much, and may God richly bless you!

Steve Turley

www.turleytalks.com

Check Out My Other Books

Below you'll find some of my other popular books that are popular on Amazon. Simply go to the links below to check them out. Alternatively, you can visit my author page on Amazon to see my other works.

- *Classical vs. Modern Education: A Vision from C.S. Lewis*
  https://www.amazon.com/Classical-vs-Modern-Education-Homeschooling-ebook/dp/B0762Q387L/
- *Stressed Out: Learn How an Ancient Christian Practice Can Relieve Stress and Overcome Anxiety*
  https://www.amazon.com/Stressed-Out-Christian-Practice-management-ebook/dp/B076GDQZMC/
- *Awakening Wonder: A Classical Guide to Truth, Goodness, and Beauty*
  https://www.amazon.com/Awakening-Wonder-Classical-Goodness-Education/dp/1600512658/
- *Worldview Guide for* A Christmas Carol
  https://www.amazon.com/Worldview-Guide-Christmas-Classics-Literature/dp/1944503862/
- *The Ritualized Revelation of the Messianic Age: Washings and Meals in Galatians and 1 Corinthians*
  https://www.amazon.com/Ritualized-Revelation-Messianic-Age-Corinthians/dp/056766385X/

If the links do not work, for whatever reason, you can simply search for these titles on the Amazon website to find them.

About www.TurleyTalks.com

Are we seeing the revitalization of Christian civilization?

For decades, the world has been dominated by a process known as globalization, an economic and political system that hollows out and erodes a culture's traditions, customs, and religions, all the while conditioning populations to rely on the expertise of a tiny class of technocrats for every aspect of their social and economic lives.

Until now.

All over the world, there's been a massive blowback against the anti-cultural processes of globalization and its secular aristocracy. From Russia to Europe and now in the U.S., citizens are rising up and reasserting their religion, culture, and nation as mechanisms of resistance against the dehumanizing tendencies of secularism and globalism.

And it's just the beginning.

The secular world is at its brink, and a new traditionalist age is rising.

Join me each week as we examine these worldwide trends, discover answers to today's toughest challenges, and together learn to live in the present in light of even better things to come.

So hop on over to www.TurleyTalks.com and have a look around. Make sure to sign-up for our weekly Email Newsletter where you'll get lots of free giveaways, private Q&As, and tons of great content. Check out our YouTube channel (www.youtube.com/c/DrSteveTurley) where you'll understand current events in light of conservative trends to help you flourish in your personal and professional life. And of course, 'Like' us on Facebook and follow us on Twitter.

Thank you so much for your support and for your part in this cultural renewal.

About the Author

Steve Turley (PhD, Durham University) is an internationally recognized scholar, speaker, and classical guitarist. He is the author of *Awakening Wonder: A Classical Guide to Truth, Goodness, and Beauty* (Classical Academic Press) and *The Ritualized Revelation of the Messianic Age: Washings and Meals in Galatians and 1 Corinthians* (T&T Clark). Steve blogs on the church, society and culture, education, and the arts at TurleyTalks.com. He is a faculty member at Tall Oaks Classical School in Bear, DE, where he teaches Theology, Greek, and Rhetoric, and Professor of Fine Arts at Eastern University. Steve lectures at universities, conferences, and churches throughout the U.S. and abroad. His research and writings have appeared in such journals as *Christianity and Literature, Calvin Theological Journal, First Things, Touchstone*, and *The Chesterton Review*. He and his wife, Akiko, have four children and live in Newark, DE, where they together enjoy fishing, gardening, and watching *Duck Dynasty* marathons.